D0277521

THE BOOK OF LOVE

RODDY LUMSDEN

THE

Book OF *Love*

BLOODAXE BOOKS

821. 91 LUM

Copyright © Roddy Lumsden 2000

ISBN: 1 85224 509 3   95491

First published 2000 by
Bloodaxe Books Ltd,
P.O. Box 1SN,
Newcastle upon Tyne NE99 1SN.

Bloodaxe Books Ltd acknowledges
the financial assistance of Northern Arts.

LEGAL NOTICE

All rights reserved. No part of this book may be
reproduced, stored in a retrieval system, or
transmitted in any form, or by any means, electronic,
mechanical, photocopying, recording or otherwise,
without prior written permission from Bloodaxe Books Ltd.

Requests to publish work from this book
must be sent to Bloodaxe Books Ltd.

Roddy Lumsden has asserted his right under
Section 77 of the Copyright, Designs and Patents Act 1988
to be identified as the author of this work.

Cover printing by J. Thomson Colour Printers Ltd, Glasgow.

Printed in Great Britain by
Cromwell Press Ltd, Trowbridge, Wiltshire.

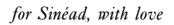

for Sinéad, with love

Acknowledgements

Acknowledgements are due to the editors of the following publications and websites where some of these poems first appeared: *Blade*, *Catalyst 3* (Salt, 2000), *Last Words* (Picador, 1999), *The Message: Crossing the Tracks Between Poetry and Pop* (Poetry Society, 1999), *Muse: The Official Magazine of The Divine Comedy*, *New Blood* (Bloodaxe Books, 1999), *New Writing Scotland*, *The North*, *Oral* (Sceptre, 1999), *Papercuts*, *Poetry Daily* (www.poems.com), *Poetry News*, *Poetry Review*, *Poetry Scotland*, The Poetry Society website (www.poetrysoc.com), *The Printer's Devil*, *Product*, *The Reater*, *Rising*, *Times Literary Supplement* and *Verse*.

'Tricks for the Barmaid' was filmed by Scottish Television for the arts programme *Don't Look Down*. 'In the Wedding Museum' was written for the wedding ceremony of Ken Boyd and Maggie Wood. 'Glasgow / Edinburgh' was commissioned by *The List* magazine. 'Makeover' was commissioned by the Salisbury Festival for the Last Words project. 'Sweltering' was originally written as part of a multimedia/CD-ROM project in collaboration with the artist Ian Birt which was exhibited in Helsinki in 1996. 'The Man I Could Have Been' was inspired by a piece in *Motor Oil Queen* by New York performance artist Cheryl B.

I would like to thank the Society of Authors for a grant from the Authors Foundation which helped me to complete this book.

A big hand to: photographer Richard Nicholson and cover stars Pooja Agarwal, Sophie Bevan, Vera di Campli San Vito, Nicki East, Hamish Ironside, Andrew Neilson and Sinéad Wilson.

Thanks to all those who helped with these poems, but particularly to A.B. (Andy) Jackson and Paul Farley who gave such thorough and expert advice during preparation of the manuscript.

Roddy Lumsden on the web: www.vitamin-p.co.uk.

Contents

II HOPSCOTCH

I.

KISS, CUDDLE OR TORTURE

In the angle of the wall by the front door of the school four writhing bodies were pressed, each with the same tousled golden-brown hair. I thought they were girls taking refuge from kiss-chasing boys. 'Are they chasing you?' I asked sympathetically. 'No, we're chasing him!' three of them yelled, and withdrew slightly so that I could see their victim pinned into the corner. As I was hanging about with the younger juniors at the gate, the three viragos captured another boy and hung on to his coat as he struggled to get free. The previous victim passed by, passing a languid hand over his brow: 'I've got a headache all over,' he said.

— IONA OPIE, *The People in the Playground*

Six months?

Dr Celena leant towards me. *Well, these estimates are never failsafe, but I should say six months, there or thereabouts. I'm sorry I can't give you better news.*

Six months? In that case, I had better stop writing love stories and start living one.

— JAY MAUD, *The Last Bolero*

Incident in a Filing Cupboard

Thank you, she says, *we both needed that*,
as if an intimacy had just occurred between us.
Old so-and-so really blew his top today, I say.
It was always going to happen, she replies.

Unless I've blacked out for a moment or two,
nothing has changed, although I am aware
of an oil-film on my lips, as if I have woken
in the arms of someone entirely unknown.

The female thigh begins a steady atrophy
from the late twenties. *These things happen.*
Male muscle tissue slackens and weakens
from 23. *I always have trouble with figures.*

It's difficult, with both of us seeing people.
One in seven of us doesn't have the father
we think we have. Only 9% of what we say
is understood in exactly the way we mean it.

Where do we go from here? That question!
I offer her a sheaf of processed application forms
like a bouquet. *All these numbers*, I say, as if
the intimacy between us had never taken place.

Because

...you write *yes* a thousand times
on the dry stone wall of me,

embroider a silver lining
in the black cloud of me,

seek out the rescue ship
through the cold lens of me,

delve deep for a lucky dip
in the sand-barrel of me,

speak your name aloud at the end
of the silent film of me;

because each day you remind me
I am the last man alive.

An Older Woman

Mid-1990s, Scotland, dead of winter
And more than old enough to be my mother.
She hailed a taxi in the city centre,
Dropped me off a hundred yards before her
And we were naked fifteen minutes later;
A Brookes & Simmons dress, her bra and knickers
Were delicate and in contrasting colours.
I didn't stop to think if there were others,
Responded prompt and proudly to her orders.
And now I wish to speak to celebrate her
Although I don't know anything about her
Except the spray of freckles on her shoulders
And that she said the world revolved around her.
I know exactly what to do without her.

Love's Young Dream

A snowball's chance in hell was what the guys
At work said. Right enough, she had the pick
Of any man in town. But what the heck,
I thought: faint heart, fair maid and all that jazz.
You've got to try. You never know your luck.
But when I called her up, she wasn't in.
I left a message on her answer-phone:
Black Bo's, I said, tonight at nine o'clock.
I splashed on Gio, creased my 615s
And gelled my hair up in an Elvis lick.
I strolled along the Cowgate and arrived
Bang on, and at the window table, there
She was! And with her, giving me the wink,
The Jewish pope, the constipated bear.

Piquant

Just as, surely, sweat is consommé
or scallions scowled in a jelly-pan
or golden acid, wrathful in a stoppered jar

and other body fluids I shan't mention
are sulphur, globster, stinkhorn, horse or Brie,
then there are these late-on summer days

when, just where nostril meets the upper lip,
a film appears, part sweat, part oil
with a perfect, clean white chocolate smell,

two parts ginger to ninety eight parts milk
and which, when I lean in to take this kiss,
says *fool for sugar*, says *mammals one and all*,

says *never again a love like this.*

Always

After the full-day's westward drive you find
the house familiar from a photograph,
its brass-hung door thrown wide.

A meeting party welcomes you: up front,
the matriarch, corn hair tied in a bunch,
the husband of few words

and, in behind two sniffly, smutty boys
you'll take a good few days to tell apart,
a gran'ma, blunt and blouse.

It's then you sense her, in and down the hall,
so vague, at first you take her for a shadow
or portrait on the wall,

the daughter who, that night, will steal in slow
to visit you with kisses coarse and sweet,
to gift you with her heat,

and who through the remainder of the week
won't speak again, although you send her notes,
whose name you never know.

And always this will whittle at your wits –
the way she gave her nightdress to the floor,
one finger to her lips

to call aboard the silence of the land
to forge the night-time colours in her hair –
until you grow unsure

of what was real and what was in the wind,
of all that being meant before and since
that single word she said.

Communion

On the ten mile stretch from Magdala to Omphalos,
they are waiting in droves to gun us down.
We always knew one day we'd go too far:

that snipy old lady we tarred and feathered,
the little blond boy we robbed and reddened
with wire wool, the hippy vegan girl we force fed

bad meat through a funnel, six days straight;
the canal will cough its secret, one of these long, hot days.
And you know the sentence, for women and children.

You. Of course, I'll always remember you.
As if our love was less noble, less true
because of these few things love made us do.

For the Birds

The whinchat loves the rich brocades
of Holbein's *Duchess of Milan*.

An albatross will stare all day
at the hairy arses of Etty's satyrs.

A keek at Rauschenberg's stuffed goat
has any sparrow creased with laughter.

And *Cornard Wood* by Constable
will keep a sooty tern amused for weeks.

As I peruse the pirls and curls
of your name scribbled a hundred times

on the back of the phone-book, I hear the *woosh*
as the condor swoops from half a mile up.

TCaLSS

When we shattered the ice with our horses' hooves,
the sea below was black and dungeon deep.

*

Late and alone in the back of a cab,
the streetlights spooling on your photograph.

*

On our first night together, I held off wolves
at the edge of the woods where you lay asleep.

Carlisle

I need to see you, and so it was
Carlisle, the halfway option,
a random hotel from a guidebook.

Her face was the moon
at the window of the mail train.
I stole a car and drove down in the dark.

The dawn wasn't planned for lovers.
Her head on my shoulder. The past,
a rose-red carcase swinging on a hook.

Chinese Water Torture

I've been noticing just recently
how nowadays, how foolishly and easily
I fall for anyone who falls for me.

I'm fairly sure that such love isn't real
but after three days tied down on The Wheel,
how glorious that first, cool drop must feel.

Response

If you shed your beauty like a coat,
I'd mope, but I could live with that.

Or if your elegance was marred,
I'd cope, though I would find it hard.

And if your hair grew thin and limp,
I'd smooth the warm gloss of your scalp.

But if they made your madness better,
I'd follow north the winter weather:

one less horror in your cast of terror.

Marmalade

As some are fooled by twenty words for snow
or think of thunder as a god's complaint,
she'll misinterpret what I'm doing now.

Mind you, it *feels* that good, for her at least,
this dog-watch dalliance, this matinée
performance of our beastly cabaret,

where cupidons join hands around the bed,
the beat-box pumping up *The Best of Stax*.
We're puppy lovers, lire millionaires;

her well-thumbed copy of *The Joy of Sex*
lies open, just beyond the underwear
atop the half-sprung jar of marmalade.

And in that moment where she reaches for
the amyl, I'll remember what you said:
don't try too hard. But it's too late by then:

she's too deep in my squiring to assess
my worth. Face facts, I could be anyone.
So, toss a coin on which will happen next

from all the oldest stories in The Book
of Love: sweet zeros, trains will rattle by,
a husband's car will pull into the drive,

we'll turn out to be twins or some such thing;
she'll pair my socks, she'll sigh, she'll wear my ring,
then leave me at the end of Chapter Five.

Sweet dreams. By all of which I mean, beware;
best know just who and where you are and why,
before you dip your fingers in the jar.

The Twelfth Kind

Sometimes, I imagine you
breaking out the baby-oil or bracing
to pull hot wax-strips from your calves,
holding a dress against you at the mirror
to think your thorough body into it,
to see what he might see.

Or else I imagine Judas,
girding the noose-knot or gauging
the staying power of an elder branch,
spending the silver on the finest bandages
to bind away her small, hard breasts,
to take her secret to the grave.

Lithium

Ten years now since I placed it on my tongue
(eight white pills of a multi-coloured thirty-one):
so much chalk-dust bittering my blood
that spasms lifted me clear off the bed.
Now, having dabbled at The World's End,
I lie here with my one-night friend.
While she slips out to pee, I check the drawer
by the bedside for condoms, finding there
instead her labelled box of those
mineral magic circles, a double dose.
Who knows what packages we keep
and carry with us? Now, I cannot sleep
in this ugly pietà, my suffersome jowl at rest
on the miscued curling stone of her breast.

Voyeur

I ask her, what's sexy? *Watching*, she says.
But watching what? Four strangers making love?
No. Seeing what you're not supposed to see?

No. Thrilling yourself in a hall of mirrors?
Glimpsing the ocean? Looking over the edge
and knowing just how easy it would be? *No*.

How about watching our awkward shape hauled
into the net at last? The gup of a toad's throat
springing back into place? *No. Just watching.*

How about watching the foreshore folding
and folding its constant hunch of luck?
The lone, long walker reaching home at last?

No. Watching a bass string throb and settle
at the end of the final song? The island ferry
returning late and empty, bumping the jetty?

The long cosh of a thaw? An advancing swarm?
No. Just watching, she says and stares
as the ocean booms beyond the window.

Her tea-green eyes. Her brazen hair.
The malt-musk of Laphroaig about her mouth.
The rutting motion of the rocking chair.

Against Naturism

I realise it's not all salad sandwiches
at pinewood picnics, endless volleyball.
I've heard the arguments that talk of shame
and how our forebears thought their bodies dirty;
how *we've all got one. Seen one, seen 'em all.*

But it's not for me, beneath my double load
of Calvinist and voyeuristic tendencies.
For me, I have to see the clothes come off:
the way a button's thumbed through cotton cloth –
a winning move in some exotic game

with no set rules but countless permutations –
or how a summer dress falls to the floor
with momentary mass and with a plash
that stirs us briefly as we ply our passion;
a hand pushed through the coldness of a zip,

three fingertips that follow down the spine
to where a clasp is neatly spun undone
amidkiss, by prime legerdemain
and who cares that it happens once in four
and never, never on the first undressing,

it must be better than a foreskin snagged
on gorse thorns or a cold, fat nipple jammed
in the scissor drawer, the bounty and the blessing,
the mystery of nakedness reduced
till on a par with go-go palaces

where goosebumped, grinding strippers strut their stuff
in the birthday clothes of backstreet empresses,
down on a par with the oncologist
who gropes for lumps, the night-morgue man who clips
his nails amongst the naked, bin-bagged stiffs.

So, stranger, what I want to say is this:
if you're to join me in a little sinning
(and this is my place up here on the right),
please understand I'd value some reluctance,
a cold-feet shiver, as in the beginning

when Eve discovered modesty and slipped
in and out of something comfortable.
For there are many ways to skin a cat,
but ours is human nature – things come off
so rarely. Come in. Let me take your coat.

Troilism

I could mention X, locked naked
in the spare room by two so taken
with each other, they no longer needed him,

or Y who, with an erection in either hand,
said she felt like she was skiing,
or Z who woke in a hotel bed in a maze

of shattered champagne glass
between two hazy girls, his wallet light.
Me? I never tried it, though like many

I thought and thought about it
until a small moon rose above a harvest field,
which was satisfying, in its own way, enough.

Theft

It's the things people say: *the worm will turn;*
what's meant for you won't go by you;
I have a feeling everything will be all right.

And it's the things people do: sit tight;
hold the cards close to their chest;
hold on to what memories they have.

And of course, it's me, when you wake
in the night, there in the corner of your room,
with my balaclava and my swag-sack.

It's me you'll think of again and again,
forever, innocent till proven guilty,
guilty till proven innocent, not proven.

It's all you will remember of me as I leave,
laden, through the window, still all I might be,
my future very much in front of me.

Proof

When I rest this page (*this* page)
face up on the bathtub lip,
I notice that a streak of sorry water
ups and throughs and greys the paper
till soon these words are gone.

By which we know: a bookie's slip
soaks up a thimble glass of malt;
a playing card, the philtre in a loving cup.
A summons will dry off a gutter,
a manifesto sucks one quart of milk.

Meanwhile, our banns could barely blot
a pity's weight of blood.

Tricks for the Barmaid

'*None of us are the Waltons*, Ricki Lake said that,'
I tell her, as she shuffles piles of change.

'Did you know most 1950s ice-cream vans
played *The Happy Wanderer*?' She blanks me.

'Elvis's last words were *OK, I won't.*' 'And when
will I hear yours?' she asks. We're getting somewhere now.

I do that burning matchstick trick, you know the one.
She polishes the brass taps with a yellow cloth.

I point out *cappucino* should have double c.
She chalks it in without a second glance at me.

I show my double-jointed fingers, roll my tongue
and puff my cheeks out till they're red and hold my breath

for several minutes. She tips a Smirnoff bottle up
and clips it to the optic. I know all the words

to *Baker Street* and prove it to her. She knocks off
The Scotsman Brain Game puzzle, starts to yawn.

I tell her, 'It's a long day for the devil, love.'
And it's only then I know who she reminds me of:

it's not that girl I saw in a crowd once but that girl
the girl I saw in a crowd once saw in a crowd once. See?

It's only a matter of time before she sleeps with me.

In the Wedding Museum

This is why we're here and why we've swapped
admission money for these crimson ticket stubs
the guide has torn in two. The simple hall
is kept at constant temperature; four walls
of exhibition cases, glass and oak, are lined
with printed cards. Let's take a look around.
Two jars of morning air, lids sealed with lead.
A linen sheet which graced the marriage bed.
And here's a corkboard pinned with lists of guests,
last-minute shopping lines, musicians' sets,
the florists' chit. That bar-till roll is bull's-neck thick!
This bucket's where I-can't-remember-who was sick.
The marquee poles are here and champagne flutes
are poking from each pocket of the bridegroom's suit.
The sleeping bags of those who roughed it overnight.
A burst guitar string, coiled like an ammonite.
A wishbone which, for once, split half and half.
A dozen albums filled with photographs.
The bridegroom's tie, the best man's speech, the banns,
some skewers from the barbecue, some cups and cans
and candles. Here's a freeze-dried slice of wedding cake.
And here's the dress itself, still crisp and vacuum-packed.
This clod of soil's that very billionth part of Fife
where man and woman changed to husband, wife,
a decade back. And this is why we've come
to visit this museum, ten years on,
with these two children, blushing ear to ear,
who're laughing, knowing this is why they're here.

Subject Matter

History

We're strolling on the beach and you are speaking
excitedly about the Reformation.
I'm feeling proud of my bad reputation.

You praise the power of protest songs still sung,
from memory, years after the battle's won.
I think, well, it depends which side you're on.

You talk (as one does) of Michelangelo,
while I recall the only masterworks I know:
Black Cat in a Coalmine. Chalk Cliffs in the Snow.

You're using words like *claymore, context, coracle.*
I'm crushing on a certain girl in spectacles
and minor crises we mistake for miracles.

You bore me stiff and when I look around,
I notice, stretching back along the sand,
that only one of us is leaving tracks behind.

But are they yours or mine? Well, let's be honest,
for I'm the one who lives life by this premise:
go down *in* history and not down *on* it.

Classics

I am bathing the twins while their mother
is out on the rooftops, mapping the stars.

My boy says, *Daddy, how many women
will I love before I know the blood is bad?*

My girl says, *Daddy how many men
will I love before I know the heart is black?*

You are five years old, don't you want
toys and trinkets, ketchup and toffees?

Oh my bonny spawn, my haloes,
sweet Jesus, my flesh of my flesh.

Geography

Posterity demands that I record this moment: down on my knees
in a clarty purple pinny, banging away with the *Still Fresh!* sticker
gun, half-mad with the squall of beeping scanners and the raunch
of eggs. Once, I was Edinburgh's Mr Hot and Cold Snacks, now
I'm not even a big cheese in chilled ready meals in Stamford Hill.
One of those tiny sloth-flies which live in the skins of onions keeps
settling on my scratched-raw earlobe. A fellow exile mentions that
it is snowing up the road, by which she means a skyful of wet, white
wizardry is descending on Culross, Kilconquhar and Spinkie Den.
I'm trying to remember: is it three drags in a draw or three draws
in a drag? *And don't cow's-arse the dowp!* With both sets of fingers
strapped up, broken when I thumped my sweetheart's pimp, not
even my position here in boxed cakes can be counted on.

English

The way she smooths her neck says
I cook linguini with crème fraîche and salmon.

Her one sleeve open at the cuff says
I write to father more than to mother.

The seam down the side of her jeans says
I hold the telephone *like this*.

When, at times, she walks backwards, it means
what do I care about maps and such?

A scuff on the toe of her left shoe says
the storm behind me will one day demand you.

Economics

God rue and curse the day I sold my papers,
my notes and drafts to a German academic
for fifty stinking quid, not having food
for four whole days, not having drunk in two,
not having slept all night, not thinking straight;
for thirty pounds went longways down my throat
and ten paid back a long forgotten loan
and five quid bought a fancy bite to eat
and five got wasted on a fast-black home
and with the nothing that was left, I bought
a silver ring which by a stroke of luck
was worth exactly what I'd paid for it.

German

The tug boat captain's navigations officer
will not respond to cablegrams we make to him.

We pass a pleasant morning in the guesthouse lounge,
comparing documentary procedure forms.

Walter used to be a stress dynamics tracer
and Paul, a pharmaceutical conversion clerk.

I choose not to distract them with the details of
my background in fruit flavour malted powder milk.

The port town's entertainment possibilities
include the region's first self-service grocery,

The Billiards Parlour, Pastry Goods Emporium,
Museum of The East Sea Shipping History.

Walter tells us why his middle name is Hahn
while Paul maintains his mother never gave him one.

All afternoon, our game is flipping coins into
an ashtray. Locals roast beneath a bitter sun.

Games

Peekaboo Horsey Horsey Ring a Roses The Farmer's in His Den
In and Out the Dusty Bluebells Dead Man's Fall White Horses
What's the Time Mr Wolf? Tig Stone Scissors Paper Kerbie
Ducks and Drakes Join the Crew Prisoners' Base Hide and Seek
Hopscotch One Touch Tipcat British Bulldog Chappie Knockie
Chickie Mellie Manhunt Knifie Kiss Cuddle or Torture Long
Sighs and Silences Saying Nothing's Wrong Letter Never Sent
Arriving Hours Late Playing with Her Food Darkly Hinting

Biology

How will I know you, she asks, *will you wear a rose or carry a paper?
Easy*, I tell her, *I look like the Blues Brothers – Dan Aykroyd's head
on John Belushi's body*, or so I'm told, me not having seen the film,
nor even have I heard of either of those men. But I'm learning to
place my trust in the cold hands of science. The midnight of the
following day, she sets up my semen on a microscope slide, this
being the scientist's equivalent of the post-coital cigarette (*so vulgar,
Bohemian*, she hisses, naked but for the lab-coat she has worn
throughout). When I place my eye to the lens, each sperm is going
round and round in decreasing circles, looking strangely familiar.

Modern Studies

The vulture's just a scrap of scrawn and innards
inside the pungent parka of his feathers.

To keep cool, he pisses down his legs;
he lays a single, silver-speckled egg.

A cheese can't be a Camembert until
it's been strained in a peasant woman's smalls.

How Charles and Paul Hatfield made it rain
in the torrid desert, I shall now explain

for facts and facts alone can keep us sane.

Reject the old beliefs and orthodoxies –
the moon is billy-faced, The Truth is pesky.

There's a hay-bale in the boot of every cab
in London. Maoris sailed clean round the globe

ten centuries before Sir Francis Drake.
The mongoose is descended from the snake.

To modern ears, 'Shakespeare' would sound Bostonian
and Burns like a middle-class Mancunian.

Facts, dear children, is the new religion.

II.
HOPSCOTCH

Happiness is the only sanction of life; where happiness fails,
existence remains a mad and lamentable experience.

— GEORGE SANTAYANA, *The Life of Reason*

You're never happy unless you're miserable.

— MY MOTHER (*to me*)

The Beginning of the End

When my ex-wife found magnetic north
in my sock drawer,
I forecast the beginning of the end.

She invited over the neighbour who found
the centre of gravity
thumbed below the surface in the sugarbowl.

They phoned the police who very soon
were squeezing a slew
of anti-chaos from a *Fairy Liquid* bottle.

The sniffer dogs weren't far behind them
and made a beeline for
the rug below which lay Grand Unified Theory.

Soon there were swarms of officials
tugging at the missing link,
fingering the blade-sharp end of my Möbius strip.

I knew I'd have their deaths on my conscience
when they opened up
the drying cupboard and found inside

the nine tenths of the iceberg which usually lie
below the water
which I'd been saving for a rainy day.

Census

One thing I will always remember:
the two of us rolling over and over
in the blistering grass by the hard shoulder,

while a mile up the motorway, our runaway mule
went saintly on without us – its heels
counting one-two, one-two – toward the city walls.

Acid

'She was right. I had to find something new.
There was only one thing for it.'

My mother told it straight, *London will finish you off,*
and I'd heard what Doctor Johnson said, *When a man is tired*
of London, he is tired of life, but I'd been tired of life

for fourteen years; Scotland, never thoroughly enlightened,
was gathering back its clutch of medieval wonts
and lately there had been what my doctors called a pica

(like a pregnant woman's craving to eat Twix with piccalilli
or chunks of crunchy sea-coal): I'd been guzzling vinegar,
tipping it on everything, falling for women who were

beautifully unsuitable, and hiding up wynds off the Cowgate
with a pokeful of hot chips drenched in the sacred stuff
and wrapped in the latest, not last, edition of *The Sunday Post*

where I read that in London they had found a Chardonnay
with a bouquet of vine leaves and bloomed skins, a taste
of grapes and no finish whatsoever, which clinched the deal.

Hogmanay

In the 128 Café, old hags smoke Royals
while chomping haddock à la Ruskoline.

The heel end of *Mairi's Wedding*,
then Dusty singing *Son of a Preacher Man.*

I arch against the counter, my hubris
dangling like a pocket inside-out,

where a sign announces, for one day only,
blackcurrant cheesecake at next year's prices.

Scarlet

I think of Bobby Shaftoe, lost at sea,
his buckles snagged on the wreck in the wrack,
Johnny in the ditch, one scarlet ribbon biting his neck,
who never did make it home from the fair,
Tommy Tucker singing the song of a slashed throat
and Boy Blue, found in the haycock, of whom it was said
he looked for all the world like he was sleeping, not dead.

And I think of my friends and of their friends
and theirs, sitting round the tables in Black Bo's,
not one moral left between them and I suppose
that I must soon finish this and join them,
all the things we know but cannot tell each other
about each other in this half-life of secrets,
the summer night music of now and what-comes-next.

An Outlying Station

A sea-fog like gunsmoke was cresting The Sound
and our coffee steam making the van windows misty,
the morning the crew was at last leaving town.

I say *town*, but more like a village with bells on:
the streets full of strays, houses glutted with ghosties
and squash full of fuck-ups, like Scoraig or Findhorn.

The worst part of three weeks spent watching the telly
in the one pub-cum-caff which served home brew like toffee;
a bar-bint called Morvern who gives men the willies.

Three weeks of bad drugs, badass jazz, bad religion,
the same German blonde who came on to me nightly
and clipper-scalped DJs who talked revolution.

Was I really the only one here who owned luggage?
They watched as I loaded it onto the trolley,
half the weight of their spurious, spiritual baggage.

We boarded the train at an outlying station.
I woke on the border of some brand new country;
my forehead was prickly with chill perspiration.

Glasgow

On every corner, someone's hawking hope
and dreams with plastic straps and wonky seams.

The men call the women *pridda bayba*.
The women call their menfolk Sunny Jim.

The past is slouched on fallen masonry
in togs which flatter anyone but him.

Birthday gifts are shoehorns, slaps and ashtrays.
At Xmas, biscuits are crushed in paper pokes.

A pie-faced waitress slams down in front of me
an empty plate and a mugful of holy war.

Edinburgh

The gods of ruth and succour whisk their pucks
across a plum and royal sky of glass.

Lush crops stand acock in city parks,
the arts in every nook and hearts

rise fast and free. That castle's just a dodge.
Hold out your arm for Walter Scott's syringe.

The quainted Kirk we emptied with philosophy.
Our old folks sprint, while everybody sings:

they are gold-dust, silver-haired and bronzed
and even minkers' bairns have angelwings.

East of Eden

As soon as I have caught my breath, I stop and tip
The woman's handbag out to find the usual stuff
Of greasy snibs of lipstick and prescription slips,
Phlegm-stiffened tissues, prayer cards and, sure enough,
A twee book for addresses. In the inside cover,
She's printed in a priggish hand, quite needlessly,
Her own name and address and that's all I am after –
The sixty quid in tenners is no use to me.
I dump the junk back in the bag and douse the lot
With spurts of wondrous, viscous, milky lighter fuel
(Third can today). Aflame, I bless and I salute
This bad boat as it parts the broth of the canal,
Then write the postcard. Just two words. The first is BLAME.
(I see her now.) The second is my mother's name.

Athena

Some nights, drunk with wisdom, when the moon is high,
I contemplate the work I'll be remembered by –
each image fresh as if I'd forged it yesterday:

the classic airbrush kitsch I called *Long Distance Kiss:*
a girl, high on mascara, smacks her lipsticked moue
against the telephone, the Muse of loneliness;

or the New Man, Michelangeline, in black and white,
whose new-born son is mewing on his sculpted chest:
a luminary nuzzling its satellite

and that blonde who lifts her tennis skirt up to display
one perfect buttock, as round with promise as the planet
which some day soon our children's children must inhabit.

Cryptozoology

The Beast of Goldenacre turned out to be
a tabby with a tummyful of feathers
while Mokele-Mbembe rose from the Sanga River,
a half-mile of hosepipe tangled up with reeds.

Mothman was a little chap called Keith
with a sense of humour truly all his own
and the Lawndale thunderbird came down to earth
with a thump of canvas, bamboo sticks and string.

Sasquatch, almas, mono grande,
lindorm, Tatzelwurm and yeti:
each one as fishy as the tail of that mermaid –
a publicity stunt for a Skegness chippy.

The only beast unidentified so far
is the one which tans the angels, holds black mass
and settles down to slumber in the nest
it found a space for deep inside my heart.

Bellyful

There was Archie Andrews: a ventriloquist's doll
who did his stuff on Fifties wireless shows
while on the arm of Peter Brough (who, if
he saw the irony, would never say so);

Lord Whassisname, that drunk nob with the monocle;
Lambchop, an adolescent sheep-cum-sock
and Orville, a green duck with a line in pathos
a ladies' man might give his right wrist for.

But if you know your history (and I do),
you'll know this belly-talking business goes
a long way back: before they gottled geer,
Enoch of York, it's said, could do an otter

well enough to charm a trout or two,
his left arm wedged into a wad of fur;
Oswin, whose nymphomaniac falsetto
lured his pursuers into an avalanche

and the imprisoned Mary Queen of Scots
who'd slip her puppet Lizzie out a window
and turn the air around Loch Leven blue,
reciting *The Decameron* in French.

The Boyhood of Fulcanelli

Forget the tame apprenticeship of Fabergé:
those tinsel trumperies and fine tiaras,
the brooches bound for mighty, Christian bosoms;

instead, let's take the stripling Fulcanelli
sending off his troupes of crimson ants
across a table spread with half-set nougat,

each ravenous to feast, but doomed to stick;
their tiny beaks pout upward at the sky
as the master youngster marvels at the sight;

his triumph over glass, his way with bees'-wings,
the expertise with filigree and rust;
green spider-eyes brightlight his cellar walls.

Or else his use of sugar-lacquered leeches
clinging in strips all down his sisters' arms
to turn heads at a military ball.

Fulcanelli, who, before his first shave
had split the atom, spliced the Cabala
of language, pledged his own eternal youth,

who emptied piece by piece his box of jewels
and at the bottom found a field of force
to step clean through into a truer world.

Scotoma

There are friends I've had for years who can't see it
and second cousins and casual colleagues
who come and go and look right through it

and yet it's as clear as a painted finger,
as if I suddenly broke into Inuit
or came to the door with a ship on my shoulder.

I tell them it's there and they won't stop staring;
I know by the nudging and pointing, the whispers
and most claim they always felt there was something

they weren't quite catching, a certain composure
that set the skin tingling, something unsettling,
a fifth limb or sixth sense forever sent under.

It's like a great war unrecorded in history
the name on your tongue of a nine day wonder
from decades back or a killer whose mastery

meant each of his deeds was put down to disease;
though comparisons cannot explain what it means to be
haven and host to what nobody sees

until shown. It's lodged in my brain like a bullet
which I could shoot back with a twitch or a sneeze.
Look at me.   Closer.   Now do you see it?

Solo

For once, I felt wanted, dead or alive,
the day my fame outgrew the Famous Five.

There came a time I could give no more
to the other guys in the Gang of Four

and I felt the dead weight fall from me
when I unyoked the clowns of the Crucial Three.

I considered all this as I boarded the bus
to quit the town not big enough for both of us.

One eye didn't seem so much to leave behind
as I sped to my job in the kingdom of the blind.

Pagan

Such things occur: I am driving back to Dunbar
when Shelley strips naked in the passenger seat
to show me the Celtic serpent tattoo

which twists all over the pale force of her body,
the forked tongue flicking the down of her belly.
You must put your faith in something, she says.

Yet what has she done but swap one implausible God
for a full menagerie of impossible ones?
What I believe in are those millions of moments

just before the moments when things go wrong.
I tell her of the night I spent in MacDiarmid's bed
at Brownsbank, snow thick for eerie miles each way;

how I lay and imagined him, alight and magisterial,
swaying on the open-topped night bus north through London;
how coals stirred and settled through the hours of dark.

Shelley sighs, says nothing. For the rest of the journey,
there is only the slow pall of the engine,
the occasional cawing of goddesses, the lowing of gods.

Makeover

The way my hand might fail to draw your head
starting with an oval, sketching in
two godforsaken eyeholes halfway down,
then nose and lips, a wonky chin
but still might add a perfect, painted crown
of hair, each hair, in Titian red;

is that the way the Scouse hairdresser
presided over you that day the BBC
brought you to the Kensington Hotel
to make you over,
much like a preacher scrubbing up to oversee
some Catholic or gnostic ritual?

I can imagine, by his side, at prayer,
St Cosmas and St Damian, twin brothers
and patron saints of hairdressers and barbers,
who had their heads lopped off, but felt no pain.
And representing bigger hair,
the patron saint of stylists, Mary Magdalene.

And so the cutter took his Joewell scissors
to your split ends (a pair is worth
a whole month's wages to a salon junior
with scabbed and scaly hands from endless washing).
He pegged your fringe back to the season's length,
and gave his blessing

then sat you in the climazone
and finished off the style beneath the rollerball.
The taxi man they organised to drive you home
misheard and thought you were Sinéad O'Connor.
I was in the kitchen with your dinner
and let you know you hadn't changed at all.

Show and Tell

Astrid had brought in an oxhorn
on which a sailor uncle carved her name;

Glen, a singing cricket in a jar.
By and by, the class were introduced

to copper sulphate crystals in a tube,
an urchin shell that still smelt of the sea.

When at last they came to me, my heart
beat like a vulture chick in a wren's egg.

All night long, Jesus had been whispering
the sweet words in my ear, until I knew,

but now I stood, my hands cupped empty,
pearl tears on the red puff of my cheeks;

their laughter booming down the blue hall,
shaking the little coats on their pegs.

Hobbledehoy

The market garden spread back east towards
what locals call The Honky Tonk estate.
There was that catty smell of flowering currant
in low hothouses rowed with red-hot pokers

and crimson ballerinas, dark potting sheds
where bulbs bulged, centred in loam-filled pots.
The sound of horses passing a window there
one night was a trick of stereo – a recent invention.

I stuck to mono and entertained my great aunts
with Bacharach's *I'll Never Fall in Love Again*
and trotted round them, a hand out for my fee.
A mildew foust which hangs calm in the gents

at St James, as I fasten up my spare,
has triggered this and summoned up Balmullo
on long gone Thursday nights. All's well until
this single flashback I cannot account for:

an awkward girl who is coming up by the length
of pleached hedge as I turn from the window
to grasp the tablecloth's end and pull it –
aware that I haven't yet mastered the trick.

Sweltering

The lizard balancing on red-hot sand,
the eye of the blast, the core of a grenade,

the demon in his nook, the sauna bath,
the barbecue, the bright side of the sun,

the kettle, cauldron, crematorium,
the brazier, the burning bush, the beast

in season, the lips of Mount Vesuvius:
there's none of them as hot as me today.

*

I may be thirty-five, but still I need
my teddy-bear beside me every night.

My wives and lovers just get used to him.
And there's this snub-nosed doll in the museum

you really ought to see. Some things are made
for kids that kids will never understand.

Would angels bring her to me, eyes flicked closed.
I'd carry her inside my sleeve for luck.

*

Six weeks of solid trucking and at last
today, I got the pimp's-roll to a T.

You're scratchy, beat it, says my wife in bed,
but hey, I need to grow it for the part.

I cock my thumb, the next two fingers out,
pretend to shoot the ceiling for a while.

A year from now..., I think. *A year from now...*
Some lines are harder to perfect than others.

*

A phone call from the South: for me she'll wear
the Alice band and sky blue underthings.

It's funny what they'll offer once you know
their secret, once you've prised it from the vice.

Come now, she says, but through the bedroom door
I hear my wife sigh, shifting in her sleep.

An overhead fan hums and sweeps the room,
turns to and fro the pages of my script.

*

The day's so hot, I feel like making it
with any woman other than my wife.

I'm like that sweltered fox in the museum,
all dressed up in his Cavalier costume:

a dandy Reynard roué, randy and willing
to puff his muzzle in desire's direction.

The pavement's hot enough for frying eggs,
but break one on my belly – it would frazzle.

*

At night in bed, the spirits come to life:
the vodka viscous, gin a syrup's sin.

And while I pour myself more borrowed time,
my wife plays records in the other room,

the needle close to slowing in the wax
that bit the heat of seven roasted days.

But please don't play *A Rainy Night in Georgia* –
I arch my back and pray that one has warped.

*

She tries to cool her forehead on my shoulder.
I'm trying to recall my dad's advice:

a woman should be umpteen inches shorter,
her nipples should point upwards at your ears

and that's about as much as I remember.
Well, after all these years, you'd think I'd know

how women are – a few thoughts of my own.
When she looks up, her eyes are full of tears.

*

We make love hard, we make love tenderly.
We make love tenderly, we make love hard.

Rehearsals are a drag. Day after day,
the temperature keeps rising. Now, we break

three times each hour to wash the sweat away.
I wonder what she's doing, who she's with.

For there are many businesses like showbiz:
the body's just a cinema for genes.

*

There comes a time to state the obvious
and a time for fever in the dressing room.

I strip down to the waist to wash myself.
I turn and twist my hands beneath the drier,

a Möbius strip, over, under, over.
You can't escape a fact, so here it is:

I want her but I also want my wife.
When I get home, we'll take a bath in milk.

*

My wife lies open-legged, plump at the crotch
and swollen, in her oestrus. Morning light

spills through the curtain, fills the room with red
and silhouettes me, hunched there with my script.

You won't believe some things they make me say.
In real life, no one ever says this stuff.

Her breathing makes it hard to concentrate.
Forget your lines – this whore here needs her pimp.

*

Chimera, Alptraum, cauchemar. Last night,
the vile heat brought an actor's nightmare where

all my previous characters, good and bad,
made an audience of old and bitter men

who baited me and jeered. I heard my mother
ask for her admission money back.

I must return to where it all began
and step out in the light that strikes the screen.

The Man I Could Have Been

The man I could have been works for a vital institution, *is* a vital
    institution.
Without him, walls will crumble, somewhere, paint will peel.
He takes a catch.
He is outdoorsy and says *It was a nightmare* and means the traffic.
He's happy to watch a film and stops short of living in one.

The man I could have been owns a Subaru pickup the colour of
    cherry tomatoes.
He's in the black, not in the dark.
His mother is calm.
Women keep his baby picture in the windownooks of wallets.
No one dies on him.

The man I could have been owns bits of clothes not worn by
    uncles first.
He has no need of medicine.
He walks from Powderhall to Newington in twenty minutes.
He plays the piano *a little*.
Without him, havens buckle, sickbeds bloom.

The man I could have been lives locally.
He is quietly algebraic.
Without him, granite will not glister.
And when he sees a crisis, he does not dive in feet first.
He votes, for he believes in their democracy.

The man I could have been has a sense of direction.
For him, it was never Miss Scarlet with the dagger in the kitchen.
He knows his tilth and sows his seed.
He'll make a father.
He is no maven nor a connoisseur.

The man I could have been has a season ticket at Tynecastle.
He comes in at night and puts on *The Best of U2*.
He browses.
He puts fancy stuff in his bathwater.
He doesn't lace up his life with secrets.

The man I could have been was born on a high horse.
He knows the story of the Willow Pattern.
He had a dream last night you'd want to hear about
and remembers the words to songs.
His back is a saddle where lovers have ridden.

The man I could have been has a sovereign speech in him he's
        yet to give.
He might well wrassle him a bear.
He is a man about town.
He has the exact fare on him.
Without him, motley trauma.

The man I could have been, he learns from my mistakes.
He never thought it would be you.
And no one says *he's looking rather biblical.*
He has no need of London
and walks the middle of the road for it is his.

The man I could have been is quick and clean.
He is no smalltown Jesus nor a sawdust Caesar.
Without him, salt water would enter your lungs.
He doesn't hear these endless xylophones.
That's not him lying over there.

Class

Always the bridegroom, aye,
and never the bride.
                    Common sense
was a tunnel there was light at the end of,
all those years ago.

I carry my hard-won sophistication
like a knife I am just about to throw.

Lullaby

Between the rusted anchor and the resting place

between the rattler's rattle and its fangs

between the looming steeple and the steeplechase

between the skyscape and the boomerang

between the drowsy lovers and the living dead

A to L, my love, and M to Z.

Between the tomboy's cartwheel and the carousel

between the crow's nest and the sinking sun

between amanuensis and Emmanuelle

between the cherry-popper and The One

between reveille bugle and the watershed

A to L, my love, and M to Z.

Between the night-path clearer and the highwayman

between audition piece and curtain call

between the spring's first orphan and the searing-pan

between ignition spark and wrecking ball

between the sleeping beauty and the slugabed

A to L, my love, and M to Z.

NOTES

Acid: There is a well-known and well-loved saying: 'Scotland will never be free until the last minister is strangled with the last copy of the *Sunday Post*.' The dialogue at the top comes from the film version of Irvine Welsh's *Trainspotting*.

The Boyhood of Fulcanelli: Fulcanelli was a French mystic whose alchemical experiments foretold advances in nuclear physics. It is claimed that he could change his age and appearance. He seems to have disappeared in the late 1940s, though some believe he never existed.

Scotoma: The scotoma is the blind spot in the eye or, figuratively, anything inexplicably overlooked or unrecorded.

Pagan: Hugh MacDiarmids's move from lyrics in Scots to dense poems in English was attributed by some friends, not to an ideological shift, but to a head injury sustained in a fall from the top deck of a London bus.

Sweltering: As this piece was written for an art project, it should be noted that the parts were originally written so as to be read in any sequence.

THE LIBRARY
GUILDFORD COLLEGE
of Further and Higher Education

Author Lumsden R.

Title The book of Love

Class 821.91 LUM

Accession 95491

95491

Acknowledgements

Acknowledgements are due to the editors of the following publications and websites where some of these poems first appeared: *Blade*, *Catalyst 3* (Salt, 2000), *Last Words* (Picador, 1999), *The Message: Crossing the Tracks Between Poetry and Pop* (Poetry Society, 1999), *Muse: The Official Magazine of The Divine Comedy*, *New Blood* (Bloodaxe Books, 1999), *New Writing Scotland*, *The North*, *Oral* (Sceptre, 1999), *Papercuts*, *Poetry Daily* (www.poems.com), *Poetry News*, *Poetry Review*, *Poetry Scotland*, The Poetry Society website (www.poetrysoc.com), *The Printer's Devil*, *Product*, *The Reater*, *Rising*, *Times Literary Supplement* and *Verse*.

'Tricks for the Barmaid' was filmed by Scottish Television for the arts programme *Don't Look Down*. 'In the Wedding Museum' was written for the wedding ceremony of Ken Boyd and Maggie Wood. 'Glasgow / Edinburgh' was commissioned by *The List* magazine. 'Makeover' was commissioned by the Salisbury Festival for the Last Words project. 'Sweltering' was originally written as part of a multimedia/CD-ROM project in collaboration with the artist Ian Birt which was exhibited in Helsinki in 1996. 'The Man I Could Have Been' was inspired by a piece in *Motor Oil Queen* by New York performance artist Cheryl B.

I would like to thank the Society of Authors for a grant from the Authors Foundation which helped me to complete this book.

A big hand to: photographer Richard Nicholson and cover stars Pooja Agarwal, Sophie Bevan, Vera di Campli San Vito, Nicki East, Hamish Ironside, Andrew Neilson and Sinéad Wilson.

Thanks to all those who helped with these poems, but particularly to A.B. (Andy) Jackson and Paul Farley who gave such thorough and expert advice during preparation of the manuscript.

Roddy Lumsden on the web: www.vitamin-p.co.uk.

for Sinéad, with love

RODDY LUMSDEN

THE

Book OF *Love*

BLOODAXE BOOKS

821· 91 LUM

Copyright © Roddy Lumsden 2000

ISBN: 1 85224 509 3   95491

First published 2000 by
Bloodaxe Books Ltd,
P.O. Box 1SN,
Newcastle upon Tyne NE99 1SN.

Bloodaxe Books Ltd acknowledges
the financial assistance of Northern Arts.

LEGAL NOTICE

All rights reserved. No part of this book may be
reproduced, stored in a retrieval system, or
transmitted in any form, or by any means, electronic,
mechanical, photocopying, recording or otherwise,
without prior written permission from Bloodaxe Books Ltd.

Requests to publish work from this book
must be sent to Bloodaxe Books Ltd.

Roddy Lumsden has asserted his right under
Section 77 of the Copyright, Designs and Patents Act 1988
to be identified as the author of this work.

Cover printing by J. Thomson Colour Printers Ltd, Glasgow.

Printed in Great Britain by
Cromwell Press Ltd, Trowbridge, Wiltshire.

CYNGOR CAERDYDD
COUNCIL

ACC. No: 02631090